The First Unrefueled Flight Around the World

The Story of Dick Rutan and Jeana Yeager and Their Airplane, Voyager

The First Unrefueled Flight
Around the World

The Story of Dick Rutan and Jeana Yeager
and Their Airplane, Voyager

by Richard L. Taylor

Franklin Watts
New York / Chicago / London / Toronto / Sydney
A First Book

Library of Congress Cataloging-in-Publication Data
Taylor, Richard L.
The first unrefueled flight around the world: the story of Dick Rutan and Jeana Yeager and their airplane, Voyager / Richard L. Taylor
p.   cm — (First book)
Includes bibliographical references and index.
ISBN 0-531-20176-7
1. Voyager (Airplane)—Juvenile literature. 2. Rutan, Dick—Journeys—Juvenile literature. 3. Yeager, Jeana—Journeys—Juvenile literature. 4. Flights around the world—Juvenile literature. [1. Voyager (Airplane) 2. Rutan, Dick. 3. Yeager, Jeana. 4. Flights around the world.] I. Title. II. Series.
G445.T39 1994
629.13'09—dc20   94-25967   CIP   AC

Contents

The Last Challenge

During the fourth flight on December 17, 1903, the day humans first flew, Wilbur Wright kept the *Flyer* in the air for a distance of 852 feet (259.7 m). From that point on, distance became one of the challenges for these pioneer aviators. In December 1904, the Wright brothers managed to stay in the air for a distance of 3 miles (4.8 km); a year later, their longest flight was 24 miles (38.6 km).

Aviation technology advanced rapidly in the years following World War II. Airplanes flew farther and faster, and distance records were set on a regular basis.

Sooner or later, someone would try to fly all the way around the world, and it finally happened in 1924. Four U.S. Army planes took off from Seattle, Washington, in April of that year. Two of them were destroyed in mishaps along the way, but the remaining pair returned to Seattle nearly six months later, having flown 27,000 miles (43,450 km) in sixty-nine short hops. It was the first round-the-world flight.

In 1933, Wiley Post set a new record by flying around the world in just less than eight days. Five years later, Howard Hughes cut the time to three days and nineteen hours.

Flights like these set speed records, but one huge challenge remained: flying around the world without stopping. That would have to wait until someone built

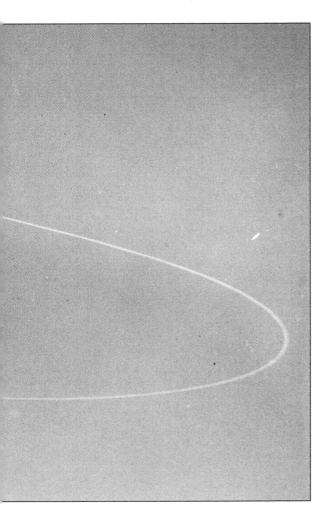

The B-29 tanker plane (the higher aircraft on the left) is refueling the B-50 bomber *Lucky Lady II*. The B-50 was refueled four times in this way as it made the first nonstop flight around the world.

an airplane that could carry enough fuel for the entire trip, or until it became practical to refuel airplanes in flight.

Aerial refueling was first demonstrated by military pilots in 1923. The tanker airplane trailed a long hose, through which gasoline was transferred to the receiver airplane flying close underneath. In 1949, a U.S. Air Force B-50 — a propeller-driven bomber — flew around the world nonstop in ninety-four hours with the help of several air-to-air refuelings.

Now the challenge of round-the-world flight had reached a new level, and the record was broken again when the eight-jet B-52 bomber became available. It could carry a tremendous amount of fuel, it was capable of being refueled in flight, and it flew very fast.

The challenge for *Voyager's* designers was to build a plane that could carry more than three times its own weight in fuel.

A B-52 flew around the world in 1957 in just forty-five hours, at an average speed of about 550 miles (885 km) per hour.

By 1986, aviation had advanced to the point where almost no firsts were left. But one challenge remained — no one had flown an airplane around the world without stopping or taking on fuel in flight.

On December 14, 1986, Dick Rutan and Jeana Yeager took off from an airfield in California in a unique airplane. It was named *Voyager,* and it returned to the same airport nine days later, the first airplane to fly around the world nonstop and unrefueled. The last challenge had been met.

Designers and Pilots

Dick Rutan and his younger brother Burt had been fascinated by airplanes for as long as they could remember, but their aviation interests took different paths as they grew up. Dick wanted nothing else but to become a jet-fighter pilot, and Burt's dream was to design and build small, efficient airplanes.

Each brother achieved his goal, and when Dick retired from the Air Force in 1975, he went to work for Burt at Mojave Airport, in the California high desert north of Los Angeles.

The Rutan Aircraft Factory was located at Mojave Airport because of good flying weather, plenty of open airspace in which to test-fly new airplanes, and because it had become a center for experimental airplanes. The designers and pilots at Mojave Airport were constantly trying out new ideas.

Burt Rutan's factory didn't make airplanes in great numbers. Instead, he sold plans to "homebuilders" —

Aircraft designer Burt Rutan (right) has a reputation for making light-weight aircraft with canards. (above) The canard is a small, secondary wing near the nose of the airplane.

pilots who wanted to make their own planes. Rutan designs were known for their light weight (a result mostly of the composite materials of which they were built), and a rather special feature — the "canard" (pronounced "ca-NARD") — a small, secondary wing located near the nose of the airplane.

Canards have been used from the very first days of aviation, including the Wright brothers' early airplanes. Just as with a conventional wing, a canard produces lift when air flows over it. By moving the control stick or wheel forward or backward, the pilot can change the angle of the canard and the amount of lift it produces, thereby controlling the up-and-down movement of the airplane's nose. A canard replaces the usual horizontal tail surface and lets the designer put the propeller at the rear of the airplane, making it more efficient.

Safety is also a big selling point — a canard-equipped airplane does not stall. When a lift-producing surface (a wing or a canard) is raised to such a high angle that the air cannot flow smoothly across it, an aerodynamic stall occurs, all lift is lost, and the airplane begins to descend . . . sometimes very rapidly. The pilot must manipulate the controls to decrease the angle before the airplane hits the ground.

In the case of a canard, the designer makes sure that the canard will always stall first, thereby lowering the nose and decreasing the angle of the wing, and the airplane is flying again — immediately. The canard is an automatic pitch regulator, and it saved the Wright brothers' lives more than once.

The Mojave Desert provides the Rutan Aircraft Factory with the wide-open space necessary for test-flying new airplanes.

The Rutan Aircraft Factory produced several models over the years, and Dick had flown all of them. They were all built of composite materials, they all used canards, and they all flew very efficiently.

But build an airplane that could fly around the world without stopping or refueling? That might not have occurred to the Rutan brothers but for an event that took place in 1962. In that year, a B-52 flew 12,519 miles (20,147 km) — almost halfway around the world — without refueling, setting a new world record for absolute distance in unrefueled flight.

In 1981, the Rutans were joined by Jeana Yeager, a young woman pilot who liked nothing better than doing things she was told couldn't be done and who didn't mind taking chances along the way. Jeana had been drawn to aviation by her fascination with helicopters and planned to fly them someday. But first she learned to fly fixed-wing airplanes and earned a private pilot's certificate in 1978. Before Jeana met the Rutans, she had also learned drafting and had taught herself about rocketry and systems engineering. Her sense of organization became a valuable asset for the pioneering around-the-world project.

Burt, Dick, and Jeana made the decision to accept the challenge . . . and go beyond. They would design and build an airplane intended for nothing other than a record-breaking flight, then Dick and Jeana would fly it around the world with no stops and no air-to-air refueling. Jeana chose the name *Voyager,* and the project was under way.

Voyager: One of a Kind

From the beginning, it was obvious that a metal airplane was out of the question. *Voyager* would have to be built almost entirely of composite materials, and Burt Rutan knew more about that than anyone else.

The secret of high strength and light weight didn't come from a designer's mind or a computer, however; it is found in nature. Using a material that's very much like paper, honeybees build a series of interconnected, six-sided cells for honey storage. When they seal the cells with a flat sheet of their "paper," the resulting structure is called a honeycomb. It's very strong and very light.

A special "sandwich" material was used for the *Voyager*. The "filling" was a honeycomb of stiff paper, the "bread" was two sheets of carbon fiber cloth. The sandwich was held together with a strong glue and cured in an oven to bond the pieces. Because there was more than one kind of material involved, the sandwich

The sandwiching of various layers of construction material helped make a large plane light. The resulting composites were used to build *Voyager*'s airframe, which weighed only 939 pounds.

was called a composite structure. *Voyager*'s entire airframe (wings, cabin, canard, fuel tanks) was built of composites and weighed only 939 pounds (426 kg).

Burt Rutan knew that *Voyager* would have to carry more than three times its own weight in fuel, and that presented serious design problems. For example, every pound of an airplane's weight must be supported in flight by a pound of upward force (lift) produced by the wings. On an ordinary airplane, the wings can be made as stiff as required to carry the load, but stiffening means added weight, and that just wouldn't do for *Voyager*.

Burt Rutan and his staffers continue construction on *Voyager*.
Construction lasted more than eighteen months.

The solution was to build a wing that would develop lift and support weight equally at any point along its span (the distance from wingtip to wingtip). With lift and weight balanced at each point, the wing needs very little stiffening. And that's exactly how *Voyager* was built. The wings turned out to be 110 feet (33.5 m) long, very thin, very flexible, and very light.

Voyager was designed to carry 1,489 gallons (5,636 liters) of gasoline. There were eight tanks on each side of the airplane, some of them built into the long, thin wings, but most of the fuel would be carried in the

Seventeen fuel tanks were fed through *Voyager*'s fuel plumbing system. The world-record flight required more than 7,000 pounds of fuel.

Voyager used two engines for its record flight. The rear engine was kept in constant use. The front engine was required only when extra thrust was necessary, for example, during takeoff and storm conditions.

round booms that also formed the attach points for the canard. Throughout the flight, fuel was pumped from these tanks into a feeder tank in the fuselage, and from there to the engines.

The flight around the world might take as long as ten or twelve days, and nobody wanted to trust one engine to run that long. So from the first stages of planning, it was decided that *Voyager* would have two engines in a push-pull arrangement — one in the front of the fuselage and one in the rear.

Both engines would be used to get the fully loaded

Not a centimeter went unused inside the crew quarters for Dick Rutan and Jeana Yeager. Imagine a telephone booth turned on its side. Then imagine living in one for nine days with a friend and a few necessities.

airplane off the ground, then the front engine would be shut down and the flight continued using only the rear engine. If something went wrong with the rear engine, the front engine could be restarted — Dick Rutan called it a "lifeboat" engine.

The propellers were specially designed for *Voyager,* with blades that could be adjusted in flight for maximum efficiency. When the front engine was shut down, its propeller blades could be "feathered," or streamlined with the airflow, to prevent unnecessary drag.

Burt Rutan's original design was a huge "flying wing" that could fly 28,000 miles (45,000 km) — more than enough to fly around the world nonstop. It had a roomy cabin, pressurized for comfort, and a real bed for the pilot who was not flying.

But as the planning continued, the "flying-wing" concept was discarded in favor of a more efficient design, and the comfortable crew quarters went with it. In its final version, *Voyager's* cabin resembled a telephone booth lying on its side. It measured 7½ feet (2.3 m) long and 2 feet (.6 m) on each side. The pilots would have to share the cabin with parachutes, food, survival kits, and radio equipment. Dick and Jeana would live and work in this tiny space for more than nine days.

The two pilots would have to change places frequently during the world-record flight, so they built a plywood mock-up of the cabin and practiced moving around and doing their jobs. To change positions, the pilot had to move the seat all the way back, then slide to the left, and the other crew member had to climb over the pilot's legs and into the seat.

Voyager Flies!

On June 22, 1984, *Voyager* lifted from the runway at Mojave Airport with Dick Rutan at the controls. He had flown a number of "first flights" in other airplanes, but this one was special — *Voyager* would be going for a world record.

Immediately after takeoff, the front engine had to be shut down because of an oil leak. The airplane was lightly loaded, so the flight continued using only the rear engine. After forty minutes of flight, Dick was convinced that although *Voyager* was difficult to control and wallowed through the air, the airplane could do the job for which it was built.

The Rutan team had proved that *Voyager* was capable of flight, but there was a lot more to learn before the world flight could be attempted. The flight-test program would be performed in two phases. Phase One would explore the range and handling qualities. Phase Two would test the engines and the pilots' ability to live in *Voyager*'s "telephone booth" for more than a week.

Voyager's copilots learned of some critical problems during their test run. It was solving these problems that made the attempt to fly around the world without refueling successful.

Early in Phase One, a dangerous aerodynamic flaw was discovered as *Voyager*'s weight was gradually increased. The long, thin wings were very flexible — they had been designed to move as much as 30 feet (9.1 m) up or down at the tips. But when the airplane encountered even light turbulence, the wings began to flap, and *Voyager* would "porpoise" through the air. The nose would rise and fall despite the pilot's control inputs.

This was a serious problem with light weights, but heavier loads required more airspeed to sustain flight, and the instability became more dangerous. If the pilot couldn't stop the flapping, or oscillations, right away, the "porpoising" would become more violent with each cycle, and *Voyager* would tear itself apart in a matter of seconds.

It was too late to redesign the airplane, so the pilots learned how to stop the oscillations before they became dangerous. After many adjustments, *Voyager*'s automatic pilot was able to handle most of the "porpoising," but Dick and Jeana knew that no matter how long it took to fly around the world, they could never relax completely.

Another of *Voyager*'s quirks showed up when it flew through a rainshower during a test flight. The canard stalled, and the airplane began to lose altitude rapidly despite Dick's efforts to control it. Very fortunately, *Voyager* flew out of the rain before it reached the ground.

The aerodynamic experts figured out that raindrops acted like solid bumps on the surface of the canard, interfering with the smooth flow of air and causing the stall. Tests in a wind tunnel revealed that the canard

These rows of tabs, which look like sharks teeth, kept *Voyager* from suddenly losing altitude.

lost 65 percent of its lift when it got wet. The problem was solved by gluing small tabs, called vortex generators, to the top of the canard. These tabs — 210 of them — caused the air close to the surface to move in a swirling pattern that kept beads of water from forming.

For two years after the first flight, *Voyager* and its crew went through a long series of test flights to make sure that the pilots and the airplanes were

Voyager set record after record. Yet another record was set during its forty-sixth test flight as *Voyager* flew 11,600 miles without refueling.

ready to fly around the world. On the forty-sixth flight, in July 1986, Dick and Jeana flew back and forth between two points on the California coast for 111 hours and 44 minutes — more than four and a half days in the air. *Voyager* flew 11,600 miles (18,670 km), farther than any other airplane had flown without refueling. Dick and Jeana set a new world record for closed-course distance.

The test program continued after the record-breaking flight. There was a serious interruption in September, when the propeller on the front engine came apart in flight. *Voyager* was grounded for two months while new props were designed and built.

Just as Charles Lindbergh had tested *The Spirit of St. Louis* before his solo flight across the Atlantic Ocean in 1927, Dick and Jeana flew *Voyager* with more and more fuel in the tanks. They had to find out how the airplane would handle when it was heavily loaded.

Charles Lindbergh had a 450-gallon fuel capacity to work with on his historic New York to Paris flight, as compared to 1,489 for *Voyager*'s world flight.

Jeana Yeager and Dick Rutan wave to reporters during one of the many press conferences preceding their historic flight.

In the first week of December 1986, *Voyager* was loaded to 8,600 pounds (3,900 kg) — 85 percent of the planned world-flight weight. It took off and flew for six hours with no problems. *Voyager* and its pilots were ready.

The World Flight Begins

To meet the requirements of an official round-the-world record, *Voyager* would have to fly at least 22,858 miles (36,786 km) (the actual distance around the equator is 24,855 miles [40,000 km]). The team chose a westbound course that would circle the earth just north of the equator.

Every pilot has to be concerned about the weather, and the longer the flight the greater the concern. In the case of *Voyager,* the weather experts for the Rutan and Yeager team had to look at forecasts all the way around the world for the next nine days. The direction and strength of the wind were important, but storms also had to be avoided. As Dick and Jeana had discovered during the test flights, the deadly porpoising was set off by rough air, so a path had to be found that would keep them out of stormy areas.

On December 13, the weather along the route of flight was acceptable, and *Voyager* was flown to

Edwards Air Force Base that afternoon. Edwards had been chosen as the starting point because of its 15,000-foot (4,572-m) runway, long enough for space shuttles to land on, and long enough for *Voyager*'s takeoff.

Now the team had to answer a big question — how much fuel should be loaded into *Voyager*'s tanks? There had to be enough for the entire trip plus a reasonable reserve, but not so much that the airplane couldn't get off the ground. Burt Rutan, the designer, recommended a total weight of 9,400 pounds (4,264 kg). Dick Rutan, the pilot, had flown the airplane sixty-seven times and felt that *Voyager* could safely carry more; so the takeoff weight was increased to 9,700 pounds (4,400 kg). When the tanks were filled, the wings drooped so far that the tips almost touched the ground.

When Dick and Jeana were settled in the cockpit, the engines were started, and *Voyager* rolled to the head of the runway for takeoff. Thirty seconds before 8:00 A.M. on December 14, 1986, Dick

Jeana Yeager and Dick Rutan pose with *Voyager* before setting off around the world.

released the brakes and *Voyager* started on its trip around the world.

But it was a slow start, slower than it should have been. *Voyager*'s speed should have increased steadily during the takeoff run, but at the first checkpoint, the airspeed was 1 knot (1 nautical mile) per hour too slow; at the second, 2 knots too slow. Unknown to the pilots,

Voyager carried 9,700 pounds of fuel. It was stored in its long, thin wings and in the round booms that formed the attach points for the canard. The weight of so much fuel caused *Voyager*'s wings to droop. During takeoff the winglets (left) broke off and were later retrieved.

the wings were bending down instead of up, and the wingtips were scraping along the runway.

Takeoff speed had been calculated at 87 knots. At that point, Dick would ease back on the control stick, the nose would rise gently, and *Voyager* would fly. Halfway down the long runway, the airspeed was 4 knots lower than planned, and the takeoff should have been stopped. But both engines were running well, and Dick was sure that *Voyager* would reach takeoff speed before the end of the runway. He decided to continue.

The airspeed crept slowly upward and finally reached 87 knots. Dick raised the nose a bit, and the wings began to lift. They bowed upward as the weight of the airplane was transferred from wheels to wings, and at 92 knots, *Voyager* was flying. The takeoff took two full minutes and used up 14,200 feet (4,328 m) of runway — the longest takeoff in the history of Edwards Air Force Base.

The winglets (small upturned portions of the wingtips) were badly damaged by being dragged for 2½ miles (4 km) and they both tore loose soon after takeoff. Luckily, the loss of the winglets caused no major problems, and the flight continued. *Voyager* turned southwest and climbed slowly to the first cruising altitude, 5,800 feet (1,768 m) above sea level.

Day One: Hawaii and Beyond

Burt Rutan and two team members in a chase plane followed close behind, checking *Voyager* and its engines for signs of trouble. When the chase plane reached the limit of its range and Burt had to turn back, Jeana wrote in her log "feet wet, we're on our own." They were over the Pacific Ocean with more than 22,000 miles (35,406 km) to fly, nearly all of it over water.

But the *Voyager* crew was not really alone. The mission-control team at Mojave Airport was only a radio call away throughout the flight. There was a doctor, a weather expert, a radio operator, and several of the people who had helped build *Voyager* and knew the airplane inside and out. Whenever problems showed up, mission control was there to help.

Several hours after sunset on the first day, *Voyager* passed a few miles south of Hilo, Hawaii. The airplane was still much too heavy to fly on one engine, and too heavy to ignore the "porpoising" problem. Dick would stay in the pilot's seat until *Voyager*'s weight was below the danger point.

Following close behind, a chase plane makes sure there are no immediate signs of engine trouble.

Day Two: Tropical Storm Marge

Satellites played an important part in the first unrefueled flight around the world. *Voyager*'s primary guidance was provided by Omega, which uses a worldwide network of very-low-frequency radio stations. But Dick and Jeana also carried an experimental Global Positioning System (GPS) that was used on occasion as a backup to Omega. GPS is a satellite system, and it was incomplete in 1986, but today GPS is up and running with twenty-one satellites in high-Earth orbit. It provides super-accurate positioning for ships, airplanes, and even trucks and cars.

But more important to the *Voyager* flight were the weather satellites. Pilots of earlier long-distance flights had to rely on their own observations and weather reports from stations scattered around the world. Forecasts were outdated as soon as they were issued, and avoiding bad weather was, at best, a guessing game.

The *Voyager* flight probably could not have been completed without the information from weather satellites. As satellite images were received in mission control, the weather experts were able to guide Dick and Jeana around storms and areas of turbulence . . . critical information for the crew of an airplane that might come apart in rough air. The satellites made it possible for the weather forecasters to "see" what was happening in real time.

Directions from the weather and communications experts headquartered at the Mojave Airport helped *Voyager*'s copilots thread the plane through the narrow corridors between storms.

And what the weather experts "saw" on the second day of the flight was a tropical storm named Marge — a pinwheel of clouds and thunderstorms hundreds of miles across, spinning counterclockwise over the Marshall Islands in the South Pacific. Marge was moving slowly northward toward another weather system, creating a narrow tunnel between the stormy areas. If *Voyager* could be guided through the tunnel, it would escape the turbulence and pick up a strong tailwind as a bonus.

Dick Rutan, still at the controls, flew carefully through the narrow corridor. Thanks to the satellite information relayed from mission control and his onboard weather radar, he was able to avoid all of the turbulence. He used Marge as a slingshot, and as the sun set at the end of the second day, *Voyager* left the storm behind and sailed on toward the Philippine Islands.

Day Three: The Autopilot Quits

By this time, the charts showed that the airplane was light enough to fly on one engine. Dick shut down the front engine, but had to restart it right away — *Voyager* wouldn't maintain altitude on the rear engine alone. Were the numbers in the flight log wrong? Probably not, because Jeana had been keeping a very accurate record of fuel use. Perhaps the engines' fuel systems had slipped out of adjustment and were using more gasoline than planned. Or maybe, when the winglets were torn off, the rough edges that remained were causing so much drag (the force that holds back an airplane in flight) that *Voyager*'s efficiency was suffering badly.

If the front engine couldn't be shut down soon, the chances of completing the flight were very small. It was a major problem, and it would be nearly two days before the mystery was solved.

In the meantime, another crisis showed up. On a normal flight in a normal airplane, the pilot can push a

Dick Rutan at the controls of *Voyager.*

button or two and the automatic pilot takes over, allowing the human pilot to turn his or her attention to other things. *Voyager,* however, wasn't normal in any respect. The autopilot would indeed fly the airplane, but every change in flight conditions — weight, airspeed, balance — meant that the autopilot had to be reset. During Dick's catnaps in the pilot's seat, Jeana would watch the autopilot very carefully, alert to the slightest sign that it was getting out of adjustment.

Several hours east of the Philippines, Jeana noticed that every now and then *Voyager* would turn a bit, then straighten itself out. She reset the autopilot whenever it wandered off, but the time periods between turns grew shorter and shorter. The problem was in the attitude indicator, a gyroscopic instrument that helps the autopilot keep the airplane flying straight and level. Before long, it had failed altogether. There was nothing to do but replace this part of the autopilot.

The *Voyager* team had prepared for this very situation. A spare attitude indicator had been installed in a corner of the instrument panel, and the pilots had practiced the replacement procedure. Jeana had to lie on her back across Dick's lap and slide up under the panel, where she could connect the spare instrument to the automatic pilot. Within a few minutes, the autopilot was fixed, and it continued to work properly for the rest of the flight.

Now there was a human problem; after three full days and nights in the pilot's seat with only occasional naps, Dick was beginning to suffer from fatigue. He had to get some sleep. Jeana would have to take over, even though *Voyager* was still very unstable and difficult to fly. Dick crawled out of the seat and fell asleep instantly. With Jeana at the controls, *Voyager* flew on past the Philippines, south of Vietnam, and across the Malay Peninsula.

Jeana Yeager demonstrates how she navigated around Dick Rutan inside *Voyager*'s cabin, which was 7¹/₂ feet long and 4 feet wide.

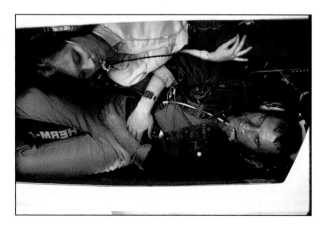

Day Four: The Indian Ocean

Voyager had to fly at least 22,858 miles (36,786 km) to set a world record, and that meant staying very close to the equator. This imaginary line around the earth is also the place where the major weather systems of the northern and southern hemispheres come together. Its formal name is the Intertropical Convergence Zone, or ITCZ, but weather experts call it the "Itch."

Weather satellite pictures show what happens in the "Itch." A band of huge thunderstorms circles the earth, some of them boiling up to heights of 50,000 or 60,000 feet (15,240 or 18,288 m) above the surface. To take advantage of the prevailing easterly winds, *Voyager* had to stay as close as possible to the "Itch" without getting into it. Dick and Jeana would be constantly dodging the storms, using a combination of what they could see from the cockpit, on-board radar, and advice from the weather team at Mojave Airport.

On the fourth day, the front engine was shut down

Occasional periods of complete darkness made *Voyager*'s reliance on its "eyes" on the ground, control central, mandatory.

again, and this time it worked — *Voyager* held its altitude with only the rear engine running.

But the big question wouldn't go away: was there enough fuel to fly all the way to California? The answer lay in the How Goes It? chart, on which the amount of fuel actually used was compared to what it should have been. Over Hawaii, *Voyager* was doing just fine, but by the time it reached the Philippine Islands, the engines were using 20 percent more fuel than planned. If they couldn't solve the problem, Dick and Jeana might have to land somewhere short of the goal.

While weather watchers helped *Voyager* chart its course through storms, map experts routed the pilots away from some treacherously high mountains.

Passing the southern tip of India, the "Itch's" thunderstorms were still a threat, but there was one piece of good news. *Voyager* was now light enough to permit a cruise speed below 82 knots, the critical speed for "porpoising." The turbulence continued, but the dreaded pitch instability and the possibility of *Voyager's* tearing itself apart were left behind for good.

10

Days Five and Six: Across Africa

About halfway between India and the coast of Africa, *Voyager* broke the record for the longest unrefueled flight. That was good news, but it didn't help the fuel situation at all. It now looked as if *Voyager* wouldn't be able to reach the Atlantic Ocean, let alone fly all the way home.

And then, as the sun rose on the fifth day and the eastern coast of Africa slid under the nose, Dick happened to look down at the clear plastic fuel-transfer valve. He saw fuel bubbling through the valve, but it was going backward. Instead of flowing into the feed tank from the wings or the boom, gasoline was flowing in the other direction.

Dick now realized that some of the fuel they'd measured so carefully had been measured twice — once when it went into the tank that supplied the engines, and again when it returned to the other tanks. That was the answer to the problem, and Dick was no longer worried about completing the flight. He recalculated the fuel load and wrote in the log, "Everything points to being 1,000 pounds heavier. We have just decided to go as far as we possibly can."

Now, well into the African continent, *Voyager* faced the longest overland distance of the flight. The moun-

This shot taken from inside *Voyager* wafting its way across the African continent.

tains of west-central Africa are among the highest in the world, and there was no way around them. So Dick and Jeana started the front engine and *Voyager* began a slow climb to 20,000 feet (6,096 m) above sea level.

From noon until sunset they had to pick their way through tremendous thunderstorms that built up all around them. Several times they had to turn completely around to find a clear path through the clouds.

Pilots need extra oxygen to keep their minds clear at 20,000 feet (6,096 m). Dick and Jeana had hooked up their oxygen equipment early in the climb, but they were both so tired that it wasn't enough. Dick became groggy and didn't feel well at all. Jeana actually lost consciousness for a short time because she wasn't getting enough oxygen.

Late in the afternoon, *Voyager* flew out into clear air and began a descent toward Africa's western coast. It would take twelve hours to reach the Atlantic Ocean, but the thunderstorms and the highest mountains were behind them. The front engine was shut down again, and the How Goes It? chart began to look better. *Voyager* was now about 8,000 miles (12,875 m) away from a new world record.

Days Seven and Eight:
Africa to Central America

Sunset on the seventh day of the flight found *Voyager* just north of the Brazilian coast, nearly all the way across the Atlantic Ocean. The "Itch" had moved a bit to the north, and now lay to the right of course.

The moon had been full for most of the trip, and had been a big help in seeing and avoiding thunderstorms. But the moon rose an hour later each night, and tonight there would be several hours of total darkness before moonlight illuminated the clouds. Dick and Jeana had to rely on radar and guidance from mission control to stay clear of the storms.

Sometimes the "Itch" develops bulges, and thunderstorms show up outside the main body of weather. Dick was watching one of these bulges on radar when suddenly the storms erupted all around *Voyager*. There was no time to turn away. The strong vertical currents

Control central monitored every aspect of the *Voyager* adventure, including those times when one of the pilots was asleep.

inside the storm cells flipped *Voyager* into a 90-degree bank — left wing pointed straight down toward the ocean — before Dick could do anything about it. The storm was in control.

In an ordinary airplane, the pilot would immediately move the flight controls all the way to the right to regain control. But this was not an ordinary airplane, and if Dick had used a normal recovery, *Voyager* would have rolled on its back and plunged into the ocean. He first had to unload the wings (take away all the lifting force) by pushing forward on the control stick and then,

Jeana Yeager at the controls of *Voyager*.

very slowly and carefully, he leveled the wings. Once again, *Voyager* had flown to the brink of disaster and turned away.

Several hours later, they were flying northwest along the South American coast when fatigue caught up with Dick. After seven days in the "telephone booth," dealing with one crisis after another, his mind gave up. All of a sudden he couldn't remember how to do anything. He felt as if he were floating in a dense fog. His fingers wouldn't turn the switches, or enter numbers in the computer, or adjust knobs.

It took Jeana a long time to convince Dick that they should change places, that all he needed was rest. He finally gave in, tumbled out of the pilot's seat, and slept for three solid hours.

During the seventh night, *Voyager* crossed Costa Rica and flew out over the Pacific Ocean, only 3,000 miles (4,828 km) from home.

Day Nine: One More Crisis

One big question remained as *Voyager* turned northwest and headed for California. Was there really enough fuel in the tanks to complete the trip?

Dick and Jeana checked each of the sixteen tanks carefully. They found two-tenths of a gallon here, half a gallon there. Every drop was important. The calculations showed that if they had 28 gallons (106 l) in the feed tank when they were 1,000 miles (1,609 km) from California, *Voyager* could make it the rest of the way.

When all the left-side tanks were emptied, Dick switched the electric pump to the right wing . . . and the pump quit. Now he had to depend on the engine-driven pump to draw fuel out of each tank. He watched for air bubbles in the clear-plastic fuel line to let him know when a tank was empty; then he could quickly switch to another tank to keep the engine running.

This procedure worked well for several hours and then, with no warning, *Voyager* got very quiet. A tank had run dry, air bubbles had filled the fuel line, and the engine quit. The only sound was air rushing by the cabin. With no power, *Voyager* began to sink toward the Pacific Ocean.

The propeller was acting like a windmill and kept the engine turning; but without fuel, it was producing no power. *Voyager* was flying at 10,000 feet (3,048 m) when the rear engine quit, and by the time Dick realized that he'd have to start the front engine, half that altitude had been lost.

Jeana read the checklist as Dick went through the engine-starting procedure. It had to be done right the first time. Now they were down to 4,000 feet (1,219 m) above the ocean. The front engine popped a few times, then quit. Dick tried again — and at 3,500 feet (1,067 m), the engine roared to life! When *Voyager* leveled out, fuel flowed by gravity to the rear engine and it started running again.

Dick couldn't bring himself to shut down the front engine after such a close call. They had enough fuel in the feed tank to make it home comfortably, so they flew the rest of the way with both engines running.

Voyager arrived over Edwards Air Force Base at 7:32 A.M. on December 23, 1986. Dick couldn't resist flying a "victory lap," then the photographers asked for

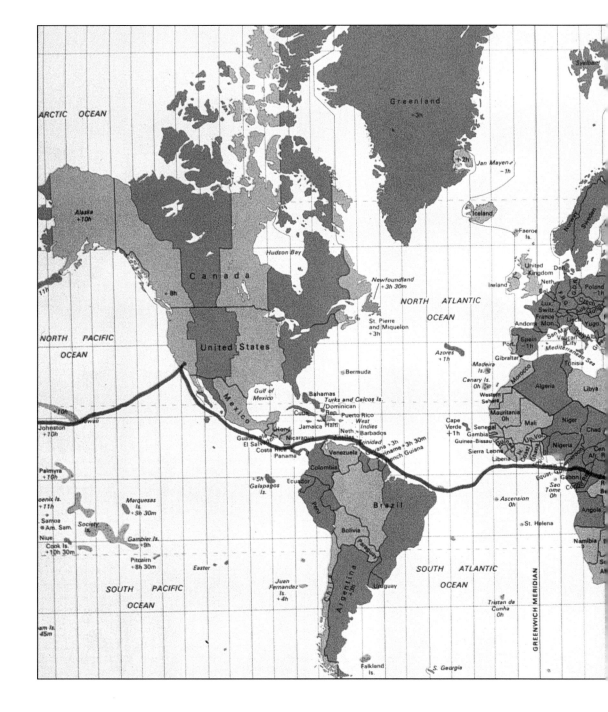

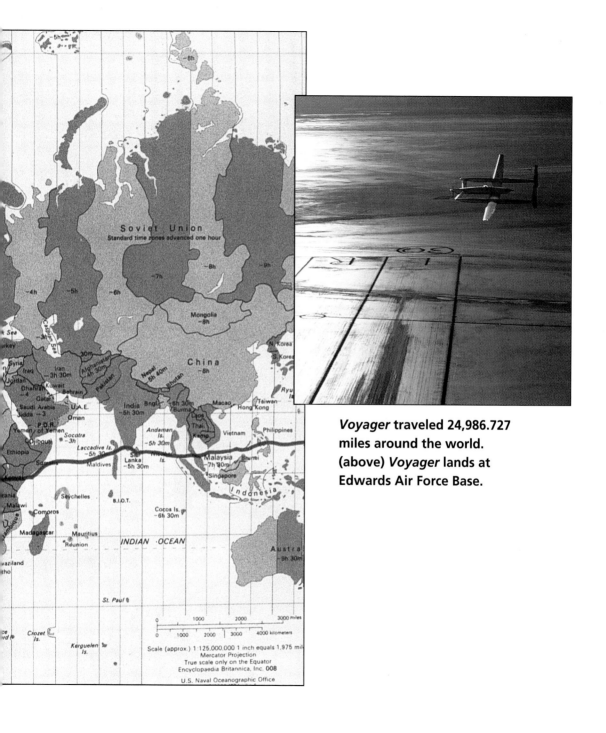

Voyager traveled 24,986.727 miles around the world. (above) *Voyager* lands at Edwards Air Force Base.

several more passes over the field. Jeana finally reminded Dick that it was time to land — the gauge on the feed tank read 8.4 gallons (31.8 l).

Voyager's wheels touched the runway a few minutes after 8:00 A.M. Dick parked the airplane in front of a crowd of family and friends who were waiting to welcome them home. Although it took a while for their legs to start working again after nine days in the tiny cabin, *Voyager*'s pilots were in surprisingly good condition.

Dick Rutan and Jeana Yeager had been in the air for nine days, three minutes, and forty-four seconds, and flown 21,713 nautical miles (40,212 km). The first unrefueled, round-the-world flight was in the record book.

After the Flight

On December 29, Dick and Jeana and Burt were summoned to Los Angeles, where President Reagan presented them with the Presidential Citizens Medal. The Rutan team also earned the Collier Trophy, aviation's most prestigious award.

Dick and Jeana flew *Voyager* back to Mojave Airport a week later. Its mission was complete, and the airplane would never fly again. One of the team members joked, "the warranty is about up — 25,000 miles [40,234 km] or ten days, whichever comes first."

In the summer of 1987, *Voyager* was dismantled and taken to the National Air and Space Museum in Washington, D.C. It is now a permanent exhibit in the South Lobby of the museum.

Facts, Figures, Important Dates

The Rutan-Yeager *Voyager*

Wingspan – 110.8 feet (33.8 m)

Length – Fuselage 25.4 feet (7.7 m)

Boom – 29.2 feet (8.9 m)

Height – 10.3 feet (3.1 m)

Weight – Empty 2,250 pounds (1,020.6 kg)
Loaded 9,694.5 pounds (4,397.4 kg)

Voyager was the largest composite airplane ever built. The airframe weighed only 939 pounds (425 kg). Construction took more than eighteen months and required more than 22,000 work hours.

First flight – 22 June 1984
Final flight – 6 January 1987

Engines: Front – Teledyne Continental O-240.
A four-cylinder, air-cooled aircraft engine of 240-cubic-inches displacement, producing 130 horsepower.

Rear – Teledyne Continental IOL-200.
A four-cylinder, liquid-cooled aircraft engine
with fuel injection. Its 200-cubic-inch displacement produces 117 horsepower. This engine
was chosen for its fuel efficiency—it uses only
.355 pounds of fuel per horsepower per hour.

The rear engine ran for the entire time with
the exception of four minutes during a fuel-
starvation problem near the end of the flight.

The front engine was used for seventy hours
and eight minutes during the initial heavy-
weight portions of the flight, for climbing
over weather, and other critical situations.

Fuel Facts

Voyager's seventeen fuel tanks could hold
8,934 pounds (4,060.9 kg) of gasoline.
For the world-record flight, the fuel load
was 7,011.5 pounds (3,181.3 kg).

When the tanks were drained after the flight,
106 pounds (48 kg) remained, enough to fly an
additional 800 miles. *Voyager* had used 98.5
percent of the fuel it carried at takeoff. One
hundred nine pounds (49.4 kg) of fuel were lost
through a leaking fuel cap on the left tip tank.

The World-Record Flight

Takeoff – 8:01:44 A.M. on Sunday, 14 December 1983

Landing – 8:05:28 A.M. on Tuesday, 23 December 1986

Total time flown – 216 hours (9 days), 3 minutes, 44 seconds

Total distance flown – 24,986.727 statute miles (40,212.239 km)

Average true airspeed – 112.221 miles (180.602 km) per hour

Average ground speed – 121.995 miles (196.331 km) per hour (true airspeed plus tailwind)

Average fuel consumption – 5.423 gallons (20.528 liters) per hour

Verified checkpoints around the world:

Edwards Air Force Base (takeoff)

Hawaiian Islands

Hat Yai, Thailand

Sumburu, Kenya

Costa Rica

Edwards Air Force Base (landing)

For Further Reading

Kaufmann, John. *Voyager, Flight Around the World.* Hillside, N.J.: Enslow Publishers, 1989.

Rosenblum, Robert A. *Aviators.* New York: Facts on File, 1992.

Yeager, Jeana, Dick Rutan, and Phil Patton. *Voyager.* Boston: G.K. Hall, 1989.

Index

About the Author

Richard L. Taylor is an associate professor emeritus in the Department of Aviation at Ohio State University, having retired in 1988 after twenty-two years as an aviation educator. At retirement, he was the Director of Flight Operations and Training, with responsibility for all flight training and university air transportation. He holds two degrees from Ohio State University: a B.S. in agriculture and an M.A. in journalism.

His first aviation book, *Instrument Flying*, was published in 1972, and continues in its third edition as one of the best-sellers in popular aviation literature. Since then, he has written five more books for pilots, and hundreds of articles and columns for aviation magazines.

Taylor began his aviation career in 1955 when he entered U.S. Air Force pilot training, and after four years on active duty continued his military activity as a reservist until retirement as a major and command pilot in 1979.

Still active as a pilot and accident investigator, as well as a writer, Taylor flies frequently for business and pleasure. His books for Franklin Watts include *First Flight*, *The First Solo Flight Around the World*, *The First Flight Across the United States*, and *The First Supersonic Flight*. He and his wife live in Dublin, a suburb of Columbus, Ohio.